MW00389334

AN INTRODUCTION TO
PROGRAMMING
IN GO

CALEB DOXSEY

An Introduction to Programming in Go
Copyright © 2012 by Caleb Doxsey

All rights reserved. No part of this book may be reproduced or transmitted in any form or by any means, electronic or mechanical, including photocopying, recording, or by any information storage and retrieval system without the written permission of the author, except where permitted by law.

ISBN: 978-1478355823

Cover art by Abigail Doxsey Anderson.

Portions of this text are reproduced from work created and shared by Google and used according to terms described in the Creative Commons 3.0 Attribution License.

Contents

1 Getting Started   **1**

   1.1 Files and Folders   2

   1.2 The Terminal   5

   1.3 Text Editors   9

   1.4 Go Tools   13

2 Your First Program   **15**

   2.1 How to Read a Go Program   17

3 Types   **23**

   3.1 Numbers   24

   3.2 Strings   29

   3.3 Booleans   31

4 Variables   **35**

   4.1 How to Name a Variable   39

   4.2 Scope   40

   4.3 Constants   43

   4.4 Defining Multiple Variables   44

   4.5 An Example Program   45

5 Control Structures   **47**

   5.1 For   48

   5.2 If   51

   5.3 Switch   55

6 Arrays, Slices and Maps   **58**

   6.1 Arrays   58

   6.2 Slices   64

   6.3 Maps   67

7 Functions   **76**

   7.1 Your Second Function   77

   7.2 Returning Multiple Values   82

   7.3 Variadic Functions   82

7.4 Closure   84

7.5 Recursion   86

7.6 Defer, Panic & Recover   88

8 Pointers   **92**

8.1 The * and & operators   93

8.2 new   94

9 Structs and Interfaces   **97**

9.1 Structs   98

9.2 Methods   101

9.3 Interfaces   104

10 Concurrency   **108**

10.1 Goroutines   108

10.2 Channels   111

11 Packages   **120**

11.1 Creating Packages   121

11.2 Documentation   124

12 Testing   **127**

13 The Core Packages   **132**

13.1 Strings   132

13.2 Input / Output   134

13.3 Files & Folders   135

13.4 Errors   140

13.5 Containers & Sort   141

13.6 Hashes & Cryptography   144

13.7 Servers   147

13.8 Parsing Command Line Arguments   155

13.9 Synchronization Primitives   156

14 Next Steps   **159**

14.1 Study the Masters   159

14.2 Make Something   160

14.3 Team Up   161

1   Getting Started

Computer programming is the art, craft and science of writing programs which define how computers operate. This book will teach you how to write computer programs using a programming language designed by Google named Go.

Go is a general purpose programming language with advanced features and a clean syntax. Because of its wide availability on a variety of platforms, its robust well-documented common library, and its focus on good software engineering principles, Go is an ideal language to learn as your first programming language.

The process we use to write software using Go (and most programming languages) is fairly straightforward:

1. Gather requirements

2. Find a solution

3. Write source code to implement the solution

4. Compile the source code into an executable

5. Run and test the program to make sure it works

This process is iterative (meaning its done many times) and the steps usually overlap. But before we write our first program in Go there are a few prerequisite concepts we need to understand.

1.1 Files and Folders

A file is a collection of data stored as a unit with a name. Modern operating systems (like Windows or Mac OSX) contain millions of files which store a large variety of different types of information – everything from text documents to executable programs to multimedia files.

All files are stored in the same way on a computer: they all have a name, a definite size (measured in bytes) and an associated type. Typically the file's type is signified by the file's extension – the part of the file name that comes after the last `.`. For example a file with the name `hello.txt` has the extension `txt` which is used to represent textual data.

Folders (also called directories) are used to group files together. They can also contain other folders. On Windows file and folder paths (locations) are represented with the \ (backslash) character, for example: `C:\Users\john\example.txt`. `example.txt` is the file name, it is contained in the folder `john`, which is itself contained in the folder `Users` which is stored on drive `C` (which represents the primary physical hard drive in Windows). On OSX (and most other operating systems) file and folder paths are represented with the `/` (forward slash) character, for example: `/Users/john/example.txt`. Like on Windows `example.txt` is the file name, it is contained in the folder `john`, which is in the folder `Users`. Unlike Windows, OSX does not specify a drive letter where the file is stored.

Windows

On Windows files and folders can be browsed using Windows Explorer (accessible by double-clicking "My Computer" or typing win+e):

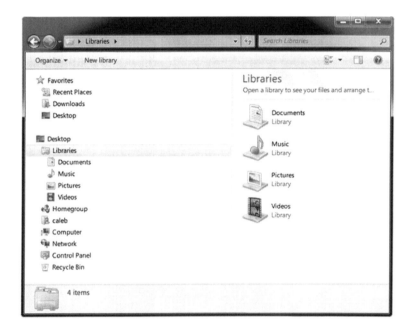

OSX

On OSX files and folders can be browsed using Finder (accessible by clicking the Finder icon – the face icon in the lower left bar):

1.2   The Terminal

Most of the interactions we have with computers today are through sophisticated graphical user interfaces (GUIs). We use keyboards, mice and touchscreens to interact with visual buttons or other types of controls that are displayed on a screen.

It wasn't always this way. Before the GUI we had the terminal – a simpler textual interface to the computer

where rather than manipulating buttons on a screen
we issued commands and received replies. We had a
conversation with the computer.

And although it might appear that most of the computing world has left behind the terminal as a relic of the
past, the truth is that the terminal is still the funda-
mental user interface used by most programming languages on most computers. The Go programming language is no different, and so before we write a program
in Go we need to have a rudimentary understanding of
how a terminal works.

Windows

In Windows the terminal (also known as the command
line) can be brought up by typing the windows key + r
(hold down the windows key then press r), typing
`cmd.exe` and hitting enter. You should see a black window appear that looks like this:

By default the command line starts in your home directory. (In my case this is `C:\Users\caleb`) You issue commands by typing them in and hitting enter. Try entering the command `dir`, which lists the contents of a directory. You should see something like this:

```
C:\Users\caleb>dir
 Volume in drive C has no label.
 Volume Serial Number is B2F5-F125
```

Followed by a list of the files and folders contained in your home directory. You can change directories by using the command `cd`. For example you probably have a folder called `Desktop`. You can see its contents by entering `cd Desktop` and then entering `dir`. To go back to your home directory you can use the special directory name `..` (two periods next to each other): `cd ..`. A single period represents the current folder (known as the working folder), so `cd .` doesn't do anything. There are a lot more commands you can use, but this should be enough to get you started.

OSX

In OSX the terminal can be reached by going to Finder → Applications → Utilities → Terminal. You should see a window like this:

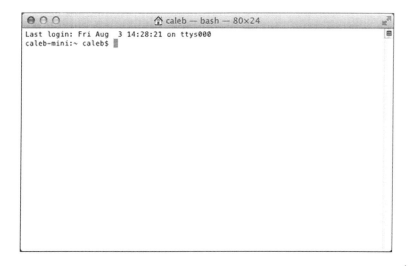

By default the terminal starts in your home directory. (In my case this is /Users/caleb) You issue commands by typing them in and hitting enter. Try entering the command ls, which lists the contents of a directory. You should see something like this:

```
caleb-min:~ caleb$ ls
Desktop      Downloads      Movies      Pictures
Documents    Library        Music       Public
```

These are the files and folders contained in your home directory (in this case there are no files). You can change directories using the `cd` command. For example you probably have a folder called `Desktop`. You can see its contents by entering `cd Desktop` and then entering `ls`. To go back to your home directory you can use the special directory name `..` (two periods next to each other): `cd ..`. A single period represents the current folder (known as the working folder), so `cd .` doesn't do anything. There are a lot more commands you can use, but this should be enough to get you started.

1.3   Text Editors

The primary tool programmers use to write software is a text editor. Text editors are similar to word processing programs (Microsoft Word, Open Office, ...) but unlike such programs they don't do any formatting, (No bold, italic, ...) instead they operate only on plain text. Both OSX and Windows come with text editors but they are highly limited and I recommend installing a better one.

To make the installation of this software easier an installer is available at the book's website: http://www.golang-book.com/. This installer will install the Go tool suite, setup environmental variables and install a text editor.

Windows

For windows the installer will install the Scite text editor. You can open it by going to Start → All Programs → Go → Scite. You should see something like this:

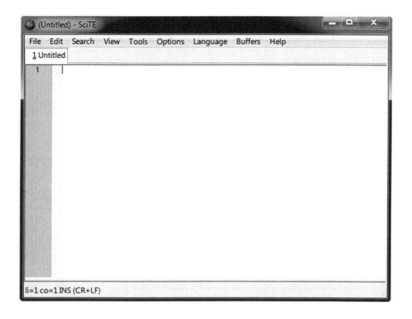

The text editor contains a large white text area where text can be entered. To the left of this text area you can see the line numbers. At the bottom of the window

is a status bar which displays information about the
file and your current location in it (right now it says
that we are on line 1, column 1, text is being inserted
normally, and we are using windows-style newlines).

You can open files by going to File → Open and brows-
ing to your desired file. Files can be saved by going to
File → Save or File → Save As.

As you work in a text editor it is useful to learn keyboard shortcuts. The menus list the shortcuts to their
right. Here are a few of the most common:

- Ctrl + S – save the current file
- Ctrl + X – cut the currently selected text (remove it
  and put it in your clipboard so it can be pasted later)
- Ctrl + C – copy the currently selected text
- Ctrl + V – paste the text currently in the clipboard
- Use the arrow keys to navigate, Home to go to the
  beginning of the line and End to go to the end of the
  line
- Hold down shift while using the arrow keys (or
  Home and End) to select text without using the
  mouse
- Ctrl + F – brings up a find in file dialog that you can
  use to search the contents of a file

OSX

For OSX the installer installs the Text Wrangler text editor:

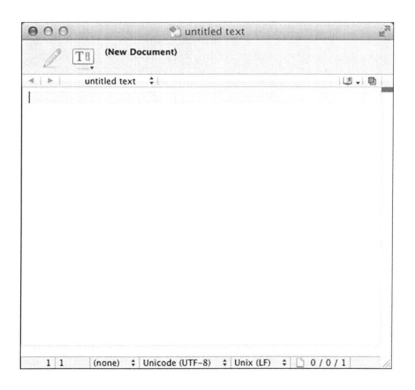

Like Scite on Windows Text Wrangler contains a large white area where text is entered. Files can be opened by going to File → Open. Files can be saved by going to File → Save or File → Save As. Here are some useful keyboard shortcuts: (Command is the ⌘ key)

- Command + S – save the current file
- Command + X – cut the currently selected text (remove it and put it in your clipboard so it can be pasted later)
- Command + C – copy the currently selected text
- Command + V – paste the text currently in the clipboard
- Use the arrow keys to navigate
- Command + F – brings up a find in file dialog that you can use to search the contents of a file

1.4   Go Tools

Go is a compiled programming language, which means source code (the code you write) is translated into a language that your computer can understand. Therefore before we can write a Go program, we need the Go compiler.

The installer will setup Go for you automatically. We will be using version 1 of the language. (More information can be found at `http://www.golang.org`)

Let's make sure everything is working. Open up a terminal and type the following:

```
go version
```

You should see the following:

```
go version go1.0.2
```

Your version number may be slightly different. If you get an error about the command not being recognized try restarting your computer.

The Go tool suite is made up of several different commands and sub-commands. A list of those commands is available by typing:

```
go help
```

We will see how they are used in subsequent chapters.

2 Your First Program

Traditionally the first program you write in any programming language is called a "Hello World" program — a program that simply outputs `Hello World` to your terminal. Let's write one using Go.

First create a new folder where we can store our program. The installer you used in chapter 1 created a folder in your home directory named `Go`. Create a folder named `~/Go/src/golang-book/chapter2`. (Where ~ means your home directory) From the terminal you can do this by entering the following commands:

```
mkdir Go/src/golang-book
mkdir Go/src/golang-book/chapter2
```

Using your text editor type in the following:

```
package main

import "fmt"

// this is a comment

func main() {
    fmt.Println("Hello World")
}
```

Make sure your file is identical to what is shown here and save it as `main.go` in the folder we just created. Open up a new terminal and type in the following:

```
cd Go/src/golang-book/chapter2
go run main.go
```

You should see `Hello World` displayed in your terminal. The `go run` command takes the subsequent files (separated by spaces), compiles them into an executable saved in a temporary directory and then runs the program. If you didn't see `Hello World` displayed you may have made a mistake when typing in the program. The Go compiler will give you hints about where the mistake lies. Like most compilers, the Go compiler is extremely pedantic and has no tolerance for mistakes.

2.1   How to Read a Go Program

Let's look at this program in more detail. Go programs are read top to bottom, left to right. (like a book) The first line says this:

```
package main
```

This is know as a "package declaration". Every Go program must start with a package declaration. Packages are Go's way of organizing and reusing code. There are two types of Go programs: executables and libraries. Executable applications are the kinds of programs that we can run directly from the terminal. (in Windows they end with `.exe`) Libraries are collections of code that we package together so that we can use them in other programs. We will explore libraries in more detail later, for now just make sure to include this line in any program you write.

The next line is a blank line. Computers represent newlines with a special character (or several characters). Newlines, spaces and tabs are known as whitespace (because you can't see them). Go mostly doesn't care about whitespace, we use it to make programs easier to read. (You could remove this line and the program would behave in exactly the same way)

Then we see this:

```
import "fmt"
```

The `import` keyword is how we include code from other
packages to use with our program. The `fmt` package
(shorthand for format) implements formatting for input and output. Given what we just learned about
packages what do you think the `fmt` package's files
would contain at the top of them?

Notice that `fmt` above is surrounded by double quotes.
The use of double quotes like this is known as a "string
literal" which is a type of "expression". In Go strings
represent a sequence of characters (letters, numbers,
symbols, ...) of a definite length. Strings are described
in more detail in the next chapter, but for now the important thing to keep in mind is that an opening "
character must eventually be followed by another "
character and anything in between the two is included
in the string. (The " character itself is not part of the
string)

The line that starts with `//` is known as a comment.
Comments are ignored by the Go compiler and are
there for your own sake (or whoever picks up the
source code for your program). Go supports two differ-

ent styles of comments: // comments in which all the text between the // and the end of the line is part of the comment and /* */ comments where everything between the *s is part of the comment. (And may include multiple lines)

After this you see a function declaration:

```go
func main() {
    fmt.Println("Hello World")
}
```

Functions are the building blocks of a Go program. They have inputs, outputs and a series of steps called statements which are executed in order. All functions start with the keyword func followed by the name of the function (main in this case), a list of zero or more "parameters" surrounded by parentheses, an optional return type and a "body" which is surrounded by curly braces. This function has no parameters, doesn't return anything and has only one statement. The name main is special because it's the function that gets called when you execute the program.

The final piece of our program is this line:

```go
    fmt.Println("Hello World")
```

This statement is made of three components. First we access another function inside of the `fmt` package called `Println` (that's the `fmt.Println` piece, `Println` means Print Line). Then we create a new string that contains `Hello World` and invoke (also known as call or execute) that function with the string as the first and only argument.

At this point we've already seen a lot of new terminology and you may be a bit overwhelmed. Sometimes its helpful to deliberately read your program out loud. One reading of the program we just wrote might go like this:

> Create a new executable program, which references the `fmt` library and contains one function called `main`. That function takes no arguments, doesn't return anything and does the following: Access the `Println` function contained inside of the `fmt` package and invoke it using one argument – the string `Hello World`.

The `Println` function does the real work in this program. You can find out more about it by typing the following in your terminal:

```
godoc fmt Println
```

Among other things you should see this:

```
Println formats using the default formats for
its operands and writes to standard output.
Spaces are always added between operands and a
newline is appended. It returns the number of
bytes written and any write error encountered.
```

Go is a very well documented programming language but this documentation can be difficult to understand unless you are already familiar with programming languages. Nevertheless the `godoc` command is extremely useful and a good place to start whenever you have a question.

Back to the function at hand, this documentation is telling you that the `Println` function will send whatever you give to it to standard output – a name for the output of the terminal you are working in. This function is what causes `Hello World` to be displayed.

In the next chapter we will explore how Go stores and represents things like `Hello World` by learning about types.

Problems

1. What is whitespace?

2. What is a comment? What are the two ways of writing a comment?

3. Our program began with `package main`. What would the files in the `fmt` package begin with?

4. We used the `Println` function defined in the `fmt` package. If we wanted to use the `Exit` function from the `os` package what would we need to do?

5. Modify the program we wrote so that instead of printing `Hello World` it prints `Hello, my name is` followed by your name.

3 Types

In the last chapter we used the data type string to store `Hello World`. Data types categorize a set of related values, describe the operations that can be done on them and define the way they are stored. Since types can be a difficult concept to grasp we will look at them from a couple different perspectives before we see how they are implemented in Go.

Philosophers sometimes make a distinction between types and tokens. For example suppose you have a dog named Max. Max is the token (a particular instance or member) and dog is the type (the general concept). "Dog" or "dogness" describes a set of properties that all dogs have in common. Although oversimplistic we might reason like this: All dogs have 4 legs, Max is a dog, therefore Max has 4 legs. Types in programming languages work in a similar way: All strings have a length, x is a string, therefore x has a length.

In mathematics we often talk about sets. For example: $\mathbb{R}$ (the set of all real numbers) or $\mathbb{N}$ (the set of all natural numbers). Each member of these sets shares properties with all the other members of the set. For example all natural numbers are associative: "for all natural numbers a, b, and c, a + (b + c) = (a + b) + c and a × (b × c) = (a × b) × c." In this way sets are similar to types in programming languages since all the values of a particular type share certain properties.

Go is a statically typed programming language. This means that variables always have a specific type and that type cannot change. Static typing may seem cumbersome at first. You'll spend a large amount of your time just trying to fix your program so that it finally compiles. But types help us reason about what our program is doing and catch a wide variety of common mistakes.

Go comes with several built-in data types which we will now look at in more detail.

3.1   Numbers

Go has several different types to represent numbers. Generally we split numbers into two different kinds: integers and floating-point numbers.

Integers

Integers – like their mathematical counterpart – are

numbers without a decimal component. (..., -3, -2, -1, 0, 1, ...) Unlike the base-10 decimal system we use to represent numbers, computers use a base-2 binary system.

Our system is made up of 10 different digits. Once we've exhausted our available digits we represent larger numbers by using 2 (then 3, 4, 5, ...) digits put next to each other. For example the number after 9 is 10, the number after 99 is 100 and so on. Computers do the same, but they only have 2 digits instead of 10. So counting looks like this: 0, 1, 10, 11, 100, 101, 110, 111 and so on. The other difference between the number system we use and the one computers use is that all of the integer types have a definite size. They only have room for a certain number of digits. So a 4 bit integer might look like this: 0000, 0001, 0010, 0011, 0100. Eventually we run out of space and most computers just wrap around to the beginning. (Which can result in some very strange behavior)

Go's integer types are: `uint8`, `uint16`, `uint32`, `uint64`, `int8`, `int16`, `int32` and `int64`. 8, 16, 32 and 64 tell us how many bits each of the types use. `uint` means "unsigned integer" while `int` means "signed integer". Unsigned integers only contain positive numbers (or zero). In addition there two alias types: `byte` which is the same as `uint8` and `rune` which is the same as `int32`. Bytes are an extremely common unit of measurement used on computers (1 byte = 8 bits, 1024 bytes = 1 kilobyte, 1024 kilobytes = 1 megabyte, ...) and therefore Go's `byte` data type is often used in the definition of other types. There are also 3 machine dependent integer types: `uint`, `int` and `uintptr`. They are machine dependent because their size depends on the type of architecture you are using.

Generally if you are working with integers you should just use the `int` type.

Floating Point Numbers

Floating point numbers are numbers that contain a decimal component (real numbers). (1.234, 123.4, 0.00001234, 12340000) Their actual representation on a computer is fairly complicated and not really necessary in order to know how to use them. So for now we need only keep the following in mind:

1. Floating point numbers are inexact. Occasionally it is not possible to represent a number. For example computing `1.01` - `0.99` results in `0.020000000000000018` — A number extremely close to what we would expect, but not exactly the same.

2. Like integers floating point numbers have a certain size (32 bit or 64 bit). Using a larger sized floating point number increases it's precision. (how many digits it can represent)

3. In addition to numbers there are several other values which can be represented: "not a number" (NaN, for things like 0/0) and positive and negative infinity. (+∞ and -∞)

Go has two floating point types: float32 and float64 (also often referred to as single precision and double precision respectively) as well as two additional types for representing complex numbers (numbers with imaginary parts): complex64 and complex128. Generally we should stick with float64 when working with floating point numbers.

Example

Let's write an example program using numbers. First create a folder called chapter3 and make a main.go file containing the following:

```
package main

import "fmt"

func main() {
    fmt.Println("1 + 1 =", 1 + 1)
}
```

If you run the program and you should see this:

```
$ go run main.go
1 + 1 = 2
```

Notice that this program is very similar to the program we wrote in chapter 2. It contains the same package line, the same import line, the same function declaration and uses the same `Println` function. This time instead of printing the string `Hello World` we print the string `1 + 1 =` followed by the result of the expression `1 + 1`. This expression is made up of three parts: the numeric literal `1` (which is of type `int`), the `+` operator (which represents addition) and another numeric literal `1`. Let's try the same thing using floating point numbers:

```
fmt.Println("1 + 1 =", 1.0 + 1.0)
```

Notice that we use the `.0` to tell Go that this is a float-

ing point number instead of an integer. Running this
program will give you the same result as before.

In addition to addition Go has several other operators:

+	addition
-	subtraction
*	multiplication
/	division
%	remainder

3.2   Strings

As we saw in chapter 2 a string is a sequence of characters with a definite length used to represent text. Go
strings are made up of individual bytes, usually one
for each character. (Characters from other languages
like Chinese are represented by more than one byte)

String literals can be created using double quotes
`"Hello World"` or back ticks `` `Hello World` ``. The difference between these is that double quoted strings cannot contain newlines and they allow special escape se-
quences. For example `\n` gets replaced with a newline
and `\t` gets replaced with a tab character.

Several common operations on strings include finding
the length of a string: len("Hello World"), accessing
an individual character in the string: "Hello
World"[1], and concatenating two strings together:
"Hello " + "World". Let's modify the program we created earlier to test these out:

```go
package main

import "fmt"

func main() {
    fmt.Println(len("Hello World"))
    fmt.Println("Hello World"[1])
    fmt.Println("Hello " + "World")
}
```

A few things to notice:

1. A space is also considered a character, so the
   string's length is 11 not 10 and the 3rd line has
   "Hello " instead of "Hello".

2. Strings are "indexed" starting at 0 not 1. [1]
   gives you the 2nd element not the 1st. Also notice
   that you see 101 instead of e when you run this
   program. This is because the character is represented by a byte (remember a byte is an
   integer).

One way to think about indexing would be to show it like this instead: `"Hello World"`$_1$. You'd read that as "The string Hello World sub 1," "The string Hello World at 1" or "The second character of the string Hello World".

3. Concatenation uses the same symbol as addition. The Go compiler figures out what to do based on the types of the arguments. Since both sides of the `+` are strings the compiler assumes you mean concatenation and not addition. (Addition is meaningless for strings)

3.3 Booleans

A boolean value (named after George Boole) is a special 1 bit integer type used to represent true and false (or on and off). Three logical operators are used with boolean values:

`&&`	and
`||`	or
`!`	not

Here is an example program showing how they can be

used:

```go
func main() {
    fmt.Println(true && true)
    fmt.Println(true && false)
    fmt.Println(true || true)
    fmt.Println(true || false)
    fmt.Println(!true)
}
```

Running this program should give you:

```
$ go run main.go
true
false
true
true
false
```

We usually use truth tables to define how these operators work:

Expression	Value
true && true	true
true && false	false
false && true	false
false && false	false

Expression	Value
true || true	true
true || false	true
false || true	true
false || false	false

Expression	Value
!true	false
!false	true

These are the simplest types included with Go and form the foundation from which all later types are built.

Problems

1. How are integers stored on a computer?

2. We know that (in base 10) the largest 1 digit number is 9 and the largest 2 digit number is 99. Given that in binary the largest 2 digit number is 11 (3), the largest 3 digit number is 111 (7) and the largest 4 digit number is 1111 (15) what's the largest 8 digit number? (*hint*: 10^1-1 = 9 and 10^2-1 = 99)

3. Although overpowered for the task you can use Go as a calculator. Write a program that computes `321325` × `424521` and prints it to the terminal. (Use the * operator for multiplication)

4. What is a string? How do you find its length?

5. What's the value of the expression `(true && false) || (false && true) || !(false && false)`?

4 Variables

Up until now we have only seen programs that use literal values (numbers, strings, etc.) but such programs aren't particularly useful. To make truly useful programs we need to learn two new concepts: variables and control flow statements. This chapter will explore variables in more detail.

A variable is a storage location, with a specific type and an associated name. Let's change the program we wrote in chapter 2 so that it uses a variable:

```
package main

import "fmt"

func main() {
    var x string = "Hello World"
    fmt.Println(x)
}
```

Notice that the string literal from the original program still appears in this program, but rather than send it directly to the Println function we assign it to a variable instead. Variables in Go are created by first using the var keyword, then specifying the variable name (x), the type (string) and finally assigning a value to the variable (Hello World). The last step is optional so an alternative way of writing the program would be like this:

```
package main

import "fmt"

func main() {
    var x string
    x = "Hello World"
    fmt.Println(x)
}
```

Variables in Go are similar to variables in algebra but there are some subtle differences:

First when we see the = symbol we have a tendency to read that as "x equals the string Hello World". There's nothing wrong with reading our program that way, but it's better to read it as "x takes the string Hello World" or "x is assigned the string Hello World". This distinction is important because (as their name would suggest) variables can change their value throughout the lifetime of a program. Try running the following:

```
package main

import "fmt"

func main() {
    var x string
    x = "first"
    fmt.Println(x)
    x = "second"
    fmt.Println(x)
}
```

In fact you can even do this:

```
var x string
x = "first "
fmt.Println(x)
x = x + "second"
fmt.Println(x)
```

This program would be nonsense if you read it like an algebraic theorem. But it makes sense if you are careful to read the program as a list of commands. When we see x = x + "second" we should read it as "assign the concatenation of the value of the variable x and the string literal second to the variable x." The right side of the = is done first and the result is then assigned to the left side of the =.

The x = x + y form is so common in programming that

Go has a special assignment statement: +=. We could
have written x = x + "second" as x += "second" and it
would have done the same thing. (Other operators can
be used the same way)

Another difference between Go and algebra is that we
use a different symbol for equality: ==. (Two equal
signs next to each other) == is an operator like + and it
returns a boolean. For example:

```
var x string = "hello"
var y string = "world"
fmt.Println(x == y)
```

This program should print false because hello is not
the same as world. On the other hand:

```
var x string = "hello"
var y string = "hello"
fmt.Println(x == y)
```

This will print true because the two strings are the
same.

Since creating a new variable with a starting value is
so common Go also supports a shorter statement:

```
x := "Hello World"
```

Notice the : before the = and that no type was speci-
fied. The type is not necessary because the Go compiler
is able to infer the type based on the literal value you
assign the variable. (Since you are assigning a string
literal, x is given the type string) The compiler can
also do inference with the var statement:

```
var x = "Hello World"
```

The same thing works for other types:

```
x := 5
fmt.Println(x)
```

Generally you should use this shorter form whenever
possible.

4.1   How to Name a Variable

Naming a variable properly is an important part of
software development. Names must start with a letter
and may contain letters, numbers or the _ (underscore)
symbol. The Go compiler doesn't care what you name a
variable so the name is meant for your (and others)

benefit. Pick names which clearly describe the variable's purpose. Suppose we had the following:

```
x := "Max"
fmt.Println("My dog's name is", x)
```

In this case x is not a very good name for a variable. A better name would be:

```
name := "Max"
fmt.Println("My dog's name is", name)
```

or even:

```
dogsName := "Max"
fmt.Println("My dog's name is", dogsName)
```

In this last case we use a special way to represent multiple words in a variable name known as lower camel case (also know as mixed case, bumpy caps, camel back or hump back). The first letter of the first word is lowercase, the first letter of the subsequent words is uppercase and all the other letters are lowercase.

4.2   Scope

Going back to the program we saw at the beginning of

the chapter:

```
package main

import "fmt"

func main() {
    var x string = "Hello World"
    fmt.Println(x)
}
```

Another way of writing this program would be like this:

```
package main

import "fmt"

var x string = "Hello World"

func main() {
    fmt.Println(x)
}
```

Notice that we moved the variable outside of the main function. This means that other functions can access this variable:

```
var x string = "Hello World"

func main() {
    fmt.Println(x)
}

func f() {
    fmt.Println(x)
}
```

The f function now has access to the x variable. Now suppose that we wrote this instead:

```
func main() {
    var x string = "Hello World"
    fmt.Println(x)
}

func f() {
    fmt.Println(x)
}
```

If you run this program you should see an error:

```
.\main.go:11: undefined: x
```

The compiler is telling you that the x variable inside of the f function doesn't exist. It only exists inside of the main function. The range of places where you are allowed to use x is called the *scope* of the variable. According to the language specification "Go is lexically scoped using blocks". Basically this means that the variable exists within the nearest curly braces { } (a block) including any nested curly braces (blocks), but not outside of them. Scope can be a little confusing at first; as we see more Go examples it should become more clear.

4.3 Constants

Go also has support for constants. Constants are basically variables whose values cannot be changed later. They are created in the same way you create variables but instead of using the `var` keyword we use the `const` keyword:

```
package main

import "fmt"

func main() {
    const x string = "Hello World"
    fmt.Println(x)
}
```

This:

```
const x string = "Hello World"
x = "Some other string"
```

Results in a compile-time error:

```
.\main.go:7: cannot assign to x
```

Constants are a good way to reuse common values in a program without writing them out each time. For example `Pi` in the `math` package is defined as a constant.

4.4 Defining Multiple Variables

Go also has another shorthand when you need to define multiple variables:

```
var (
    a = 5
    b = 10
    c = 15
)
```

Use the keyword `var` (or `const`) followed by parentheses with each variable on its own line.

4.5   An Example Program

Here's an example program which takes in a number
entered by the user and doubles it:

```go
package main

import "fmt"

func main() {
    fmt.Print("Enter a number: ")
    var input float64
    fmt.Scanf("%f", &input)

    output := input * 2

    fmt.Println(output)
}
```

We use another function from the `fmt` package to read
the user input (`Scanf`). `&input` will be explained in a
later chapter, for now all we need to know is that `Scanf`
fills input with the number we enter.

Problems

1. What are two ways to create a new variable?

2. What is the value of x after running:
   `x := 5; x += 1`?

3. What is scope and how do you determine the scope of a variable in Go?

4. What is the difference between `var` and `const`?

5. Using the example program as a starting point, write a program that converts from Fahrenheit into Celsius. (`C = (F - 32) * 5/9`)

6. Write another program that converts from feet into meters. (`1 ft = 0.3048 m`)

5   Control Structures

Now that we know how to use variables it's time to start writing some useful programs. First let's write a program that counts to 10, starting from 1, with each number on its own line. Using what we've learned so far we could write this:

```go
package main

import "fmt"

func main() {
    fmt.Println(1)
    fmt.Println(2)
    fmt.Println(3)
    fmt.Println(4)
    fmt.Println(5)
    fmt.Println(6)
    fmt.Println(7)
    fmt.Println(8)
    fmt.Println(9)
    fmt.Println(10)
}
```

Or this:

```
package main
import "fmt"

func main() {
    fmt.Println(`1
2
3
4
5
6
7
8
9
10`)
}
```

But both of these programs are pretty tedious to write. What we need is a way of doing something multiple times.

5.1 For

The for statement allows us to repeat a list of statements (a block) multiple times. Rewriting our previous program using a for statement looks like this:

```
package main

import "fmt"

func main() {
    i := 1
    for i <= 10 {
        fmt.Println(i)
        i = i + 1
    }
}
```

First we create a variable called `i` that we use to store the number we want to print. Then we create a `for` loop by using the keyword `for`, providing a conditional expression which is either `true` or `false` and finally supplying a block to execute. The for loop works like this:

1. We evaluate (run) the expression `i <= 10` ("i less than or equal to 10"). If this evaluates to true then we run the statements inside of the block. Otherwise we jump to the next line of our program after the block. (in this case there is nothing after the for loop so we exit the program)

2. After we run the statements inside of the block we loop back to the beginning of the for statement and repeat step 1.

The `i = i + 1` line is extremely important, because
without it `i <= 10` would always evaluate to `true` and
our program would never stop. (When this happens
this is referred to as an infinite loop)

As an exercise lets walk through the program like a
computer would:

- Create a variable named `i` with the value 1
- Is `i <= 10`? Yes.
- Print `i`
- Set `i` to `i + 1` (`i` now equals 2)
- Is `i <= 10`? Yes.
- Print `i`
- Set `i` to `i + 1` (`i` now equals 3)
- ...
- Set `i` to `i + 1` (`i` now equals 11)
- Is `i <= 10`? No.
- Nothing left to do, so exit

Other programming languages have a lot of different
types of loops (while, do, until, foreach, ...) but Go only
has one that can be used in a variety of different ways.
The previous program could also have been written
like this:

```
func main() {
    for i := 1; i <= 10; i++ {
        fmt.Println(i)
    }
}
```

Now the conditional expression also contains two other statements with semicolons between them. First we have the variable initialization, then we have the condition to check each time and finally we "increment" the variable. (adding 1 to a variable is so common that we have a special operator: ++. Similarly subtracting 1 can be done with --)

We will see additional ways of using the for loop in later chapters.

5.2   If

Let's modify the program we just wrote so that instead of just printing the numbers 1-10 on each line it also specifies whether or not the number is even or odd. Like this:

```
1 odd
2 even
3 odd
4 even
5 odd
6 even
7 odd
8 even
9 odd
10 even
```

First we need a way of determining whether or not a number is even or odd. An easy way to tell is to divide the number by 2. If you have nothing left over then the number is even, otherwise it's odd. So how do we find the remainder after division in Go? We use the % operator. 1 % 2 equals 1, 2 % 2 equals 0, 3 % 2 equals 1 and so on.

Next we need a way of choosing to do different things based on a condition. For that we use the if statement:

```
if i % 2 == 0 {
  // even
} else {
  // odd
}
```

An if statement is similar to a for statement in that it

has a condition followed by a block. If statements also have an optional `else` part. If the condition evaluates to `true` then the block after the condition is run, otherwise either the block is skipped or if the `else` block is present that block is run.

If statements can also have `else if` parts:

```
if i % 2 == 0 {
    // divisible by 2
} else if i % 3 == 0 {
    // divisible by 3
} else if i % 4 == 0 {
    // divisible by 4
}
```

The conditions are checked top down and the first one to result in true will have its associated block executed. None of the other blocks will execute, even if their conditions also pass. (So for example the number 8 is divisible by both 4 and 2, but the `// divisible by 4` block will never execute because the `// divisible by 2` block is done first)

Putting it all together we have:

```
func main() {
    for i := 1; i <= 10; i++ {
        if i % 2 == 0 {
            fmt.Println(i, "even")
        } else {
            fmt.Println(i, "odd")
        }
    }
}
```

Let's walk through this program:

- Create a variable i of type int and give it the value 1
- Is i less than or equal to 10? Yes: jump to the block
- Is the remainder of i ÷ 2 equal to 0? No: jump to the else block
- Print i followed by odd
- Increment i (the statement after the condition)
- Is i less than or equal to 10? Yes: jump to the block
- Is the remainder of i ÷ 2 equal to 0? Yes: jump to the if block
- Print i followed by even
- ...

The remainder operator, while rarely seen outside of elementary school, turns out to be really useful when programming. You'll see it turn up everywhere from zebra striping tables to partitioning data sets.

5.3   Switch

Suppose we wanted to write a program that printed the English names for numbers. Using what we've learned so far we might start by doing this:

```go
if i == 0 {
    fmt.Println("Zero")
} else if i == 1 {
    fmt.Println("One")
} else if i == 2 {
    fmt.Println("Two")
} else if i == 3 {
    fmt.Println("Three")
} else if i == 4 {
    fmt.Println("Four")
} else if i == 5 {
    fmt.Println("Five")
}
```

Since writing a program in this way would be pretty tedious Go provides another statement to make this easier: the `switch` statement. We can rewrite our program to look like this:

```
switch i {
case 0: fmt.Println("Zero")
case 1: fmt.Println("One")
case 2: fmt.Println("Two")
case 3: fmt.Println("Three")
case 4: fmt.Println("Four")
case 5: fmt.Println("Five")
default: fmt.Println("Unknown Number")
}
```

A switch statement starts with the keyword `switch` followed by an expression (in this case `i`) and then a series of `cases`. The value of the expression is compared to the expression following each `case` keyword. If they are equivalent then the statement(s) following the `:` is executed.

Like an if statement each case is checked top down and the first one to succeed is chosen. A switch also supports a default case which will happen if none of the cases matches the value. (Kind of like the else in an if statement)

These are the main control flow statements. Additional statements will be explored in later chapters.

Problems

1. What does the following program print:

```
i := 10
if i > 10 {
    fmt.Println("Big")
} else {
    fmt.Println("Small")
}
```

2. Write a program that prints out all the numbers evenly divisible by 3 between 1 and 100. (3, 6, 9, etc.)

3. Write a program that prints the numbers from 1 to 100. But for multiples of three print "Fizz" instead of the number and for the multiples of five print "Buzz". For numbers which are multiples of both three and five print "FizzBuzz".

6   Arrays, Slices and Maps

In chapter 3 we learned about Go's basic types. In this chapter we will look at three more built-in types: arrays, slices and maps.

6.1   Arrays

An array is a numbered sequence of elements of a single type with a fixed length. In Go they look like this:

```
var x [5]int
```

x is an example of an array which is composed of 5 ints. Try running the following program:

```
package main

import "fmt"

func main() {
    var x [5]int
    x[4] = 100
    fmt.Println(x)
}
```

You should see this:

```
[0 0 0 0 100]
```

x[4] = 100 should be read "set the 5th element of the
array x to 100". It might seem strange that x[4] represents the 5th element instead of the 4th but like strings,
arrays are indexed starting from 0. Arrays are accessed in a similar way. We could change
fmt.Println(x) to fmt.Println(x[4]) and we would get
100.

Here's an example program that uses arrays:

```
func main() {
    var x [5]float64
    x[0] = 98
    x[1] = 93
    x[2] = 77
    x[3] = 82
    x[4] = 83

    var total float64 = 0
    for i := 0; i < 5; i++ {
        total += x[i]
    }
    fmt.Println(total / 5)
}
```

This program computes the average of a series of test scores. If you run it you should see `86.6`. Let's walk through the program:

- First we create an array of length 5 to hold our test scores, then we fill up each element with a grade
- Next we setup a for loop to compute the total score
- Finally we divide the total score by the number of elements to find the average

This program works, but Go provides some features we can use to improve it. First these 2 parts: `i < 5` and `total / 5` should throw up a red flag for us. Say we changed the number of grades from 5 to 6. We would also need to change both of these parts. It would be better to use the length of the array instead:

```go
var total float64 = 0
for i := 0; i < len(x); i++ {
    total += x[i]
}
fmt.Println(total / len(x))
```

Go ahead and make these changes and run the program. You should get an error:

```
$ go run tmp.go
# command-line-arguments
.\tmp.go:19: invalid operation: total / 5
(mismatched types float64 and int)
```

The issue here is that `len(x)` and `total` have different types. `total` is a `float64` while `len(x)` is an `int`. So we need to convert `len(x)` into a `float64`:

```go
fmt.Println(total / float64(len(x)))
```

This is an example of a type conversion. In general to convert between types you use the type name like a function.

Another change to the program we can make is to use
a special form of the for loop:

```
var total float64 = 0
for i, value := range x {
    total += value
}
fmt.Println(total / float64(len(x)))
```

In this for loop `i` represents the current position in the
array and `value` is the same as `x[i]`. We use the keyword `range` followed by the name of the variable we
want to loop over.

Running this program will result in another error:

```
$ go run tmp.go
# command-line-arguments
.\tmp.go:16: i declared and not used
```

The Go compiler won't allow you to create variables
that you never use. Since we don't use `i` inside of our
loop we need to change it to this:

```
var total float64 = 0
for _, value := range x {
    total += value
}
fmt.Println(total / float64(len(x)))
```

A single _ (underscore) is used to tell the compiler that
we don't need this. (In this case we don't need the iter-
ator variable)

Go also provides a shorter syntax for creating arrays:

```
x := [5]float64{ 98, 93, 77, 82, 83 }
```

We no longer need to specify the type because Go can
figure it out. Sometimes arrays like this can get too
long to fit on one line, so Go allows you to break it up
like this:

```
x := [5]float64{
    98,
    93,
    77,
    82,
    83,
}
```

Notice the extra trailing , after 83. This is required by

Go and it allows us to easily remove an element from
the array by commenting out the line:

```
x := [4]float64{
    98,
    93,
    77,
    82,
    // 83,
}
```

This example illustrates a major issue with arrays:
their length is fixed and part of the array's type name.
In order to remove the last item, we actually had to
change the type as well. Go's solution to this problem
is to use a different type: slices.

6.2   Slices

A slice is a segment of an array. Like arrays slices are
indexable and have a length. Unlike arrays this length
is allowed to change. Here's an example of a slice:

```
var x []float64
```

The only difference between this and an array is the
missing length between the brackets. In this case x
has been created with a length of 0.

If you want to create a slice you should use the built-in `make` function:

```
x := make([]float64, 5)
```

This creates a slice that is associated with an underlying `float64` array of length 5. Slices are always associated with some array, and although they can never be longer than the array, they can be smaller. The `make` function also allows a 3rd parameter:

```
x := make([]float64, 5, 10)
```

10 represents the capacity of the underlying array which the slice points to:

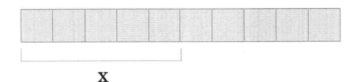

X

Another way to create slices is to use the `[low : high]` expression:

```
arr := []float64{1,2,3,4,5}
x := arr[0:5]
```

`low` is the index of where to start the slice and `high` is the index where to end it (but not including the index itself). For example while `arr[0:5]` returns `[1,2,3,4,5]`, `arr[1:4]` returns `[2,3,4]`.

For convenience we are also allowed to omit `low`, `high` or even both `low` and `high`. `arr[0:]` is the same as `arr[0:len(arr)]`, `arr[:5]` is the same as `arr[0:5]` and `arr[:]` is the same as `arr[0:len(arr)]`.

Slice Functions

Go includes two built-in functions to assist with slices: `append` and `copy`. Here is an example of `append`:

```
func main() {
    slice1 := []int{1,2,3}
    slice2 := append(slice1, 4, 5)
    fmt.Println(slice1, slice2)
}
```

After running this program `slice1` has `[1,2,3]` and `slice2` has `[1,2,3,4,5]`. `append` creates a new slice by taking an existing slice (the first argument) and appending all the following arguments to it.

Here is an example of copy:

```
func main() {
    slice1 := []int{1,2,3}
    slice2 := make([]int, 2)
    copy(slice2, slice1)
    fmt.Println(slice1, slice2)
}
```

After running this program `slice1` has `[1,2,3]` and `slice2` has `[1,2]`. The contents of `slice1` are copied into `slice2`, but since `slice2` has room for only two elements only the first two elements of `slice1` are copied.

6.3   Maps

A map is an unordered collection of key-value pairs. Also known as an associative array, a hash table or a dictionary, maps are used to look up a value by its associated key. Here's an example of a map in Go:

```
var x map[string]int
```

The map type is represented by the keyword `map`, followed by the key type in brackets and finally the value type. If you were to read this out loud you would say "`x` is a map of `strings` to `ints`."

Like arrays and slices maps can be accessed using brackets. Try running the following program:

```
var x map[string]int
x["key"] = 10
fmt.Println(x)
```

You should see an error similar to this:

```
panic: runtime error: assignment to entry in nil
map

goroutine 1 [running]:
main.main()
  main.go:7 +0x4d

goroutine 2 [syscall]:
created by runtime.main

C:/Users/ADMINI~1/AppData/Local/Temp/2/bindi
t269497170/go/src/pkg/runtime/proc.c:221
exit status 2
```

Up till now we have only seen compile-time errors. This is an example of a runtime error. As the name would imply, runtime errors happen when you run the program, while compile-time errors happen when you try to compile the program.

The problem with our program is that maps have to be initialized before they can be used. We should have written this:

```
x := make(map[string]int)
x["key"] = 10
fmt.Println(x["key"])
```

If you run this program you should see `10` displayed.
The statement `x["key"] = 10` is similar to what we
saw with arrays but the key, instead of being an integer, is a string because the map's key type is `string`.
We can also create maps with a key type of `int`:

```
x := make(map[int]int)
x[1] = 10
fmt.Println(x[1])
```

This looks very much like an array but there are a few
differences. First the length of a map (found by doing
`len(x)`) can change as we add new items to it. When
first created it has a length of 0, after `x[1] = 10` it has
a length of 1. Second maps are not sequential. We have
`x[1]`, and with an array that would imply there must
be an `x[0]`, but maps don't have this requirement.

We can also delete items from a map using the built-in
`delete` function:

```
delete(x, 1)
```

Let's look at an example program that uses a map:

```
package main

import "fmt"

func main() {
    elements := make(map[string]string)
    elements["H"] = "Hydrogen"
    elements["He"] = "Helium"
    elements["Li"] = "Lithium"
    elements["Be"] = "Beryllium"
    elements["B"] = "Boron"
    elements["C"] = "Carbon"
    elements["N"] = "Nitrogen"
    elements["O"] = "Oxygen"
    elements["F"] = "Fluorine"
    elements["Ne"] = "Neon"

    fmt.Println(elements["Li"])
}
```

`elements` is a map that represents the first 10 chemical elements indexed by their symbol. This is a very common way of using maps: as a lookup table or a dictionary. Suppose we tried to look up an element that doesn't exist:

```
fmt.Println(elements["Un"])
```

If you run this you should see nothing returned. Technically a map returns the zero value for the value type (which for strings is the empty string). Although we could check for the zero value in a condition (`elements["Un"] == ""`) Go provides a better way:

```
name, ok := elements["Un"]
fmt.Println(name, ok)
```

Accessing an element of a map can return two values instead of just one. The first value is the result of the lookup, the second tells us whether or not the lookup was successful. In Go we often see code like this:

```
if name, ok := elements["Un"]; ok {
    fmt.Println(name, ok)
}
```

First we try to get the value from the map, then if it's successful we run the code inside of the block.

Like we saw with arrays there is also a shorter way to create maps:

```
elements := map[string]string{
    "H": "Hydrogen",
    "He": "Helium",
    "Li": "Lithium",
    "Be": "Beryllium",
    "B": "Boron",
    "C": "Carbon",
    "N": "Nitrogen",
    "O": "Oxygen",
    "F": "Fluorine",
    "Ne": "Neon",
}
```

Maps are also often used to store general information. Let's modify our program so that instead of just storing the name of the element we store its standard state (state at room temperature) as well:

```
func main() {
    elements := map[string]map[string]string{
        "H": map[string]string{
            "name":"Hydrogen",
            "state":"gas",
        },
        "He": map[string]string{
            "name":"Helium",
            "state":"gas",
        },
        "Li": map[string]string{
            "name":"Lithium",
            "state":"solid",
        },
```

```
        "Be":  map[string]string{
                "name":"Beryllium",
                "state":"solid",
        },
        "B":   map[string]string{
                "name":"Boron",
                "state":"solid",
        },
        "C":   map[string]string{
                "name":"Carbon",
                "state":"solid",
        },
        "N":   map[string]string{
                "name":"Nitrogen",
                "state":"gas",
        },
        "O":   map[string]string{
                "name":"Oxygen",
                "state":"gas",
        },
        "F":   map[string]string{
                "name":"Fluorine",
                "state":"gas",
        },
        "Ne":  map[string]string{
                "name":"Neon",
                "state":"gas",
        },
    }

    if el, ok := elements["Li"]; ok {
        fmt.Println(el["name"], el["state"])
    }
}
```

Notice that the type of our map has changed from

`map[string]string` to `map[string]map[string]string`. We now have a map of strings to maps of strings to strings. The outer map is used as a lookup table based on the element's symbol, while the inner maps are used to store general information about the elements. Although maps are often used like this, in chapter 9 we will see a better way to store structured information.

Problems

1. How do you access the 4th element of an array or slice?

1. How do you access the 4th element of an array or slice?

2. What is the length of a slice created using: `make([]int, 3, 9)`?

3. Given the array:

```
x := [6]string{"a","b","c","d","e","f"}
```

what would `x[2:5]` give you?

4. Write a program that finds the smallest number in this list:

```
x := []int{
    48,96,86,68,
    57,82,63,70,
    37,34,83,27,
    19,97, 9,17,
}
```

7 Functions

A function is an independent section of code that maps zero or more input parameters to zero or more output parameters. Functions (also known as procedures or subroutines) are often represented as a black box: (the black box represents the function)

Inputs ——▶   ——▶ Outputs

Until now the programs we have written in Go have used only one function:

```
func main() {}
```

We will now begin writing programs that use more than one function.

7.1   Your Second Function

Remember this program from chapter 6:

```
func main() {
    xs := []float64{98,93,77,82,83}

    total := 0.0
    for _, v := range xs {
        total += v
    }
    fmt.Println(total / float64(len(xs)))
}
```

This program computes the average of a series of numbers. Finding the average like this is a very general
problem, so its an ideal candidate for definition as a
function.

The `average` function will need to take in a slice of
`float64`s and return one `float64`. Insert this before the
`main` function:

```
func average(xs []float64) float64 {
    panic("Not Implemented")
}
```

Functions start with the keyword `func`, followed by the
function's name. The parameters (inputs) of the func-

tion are defined like this: `name type, name type, ....`
Our function has one parameter (the list of scores) that
we named `xs`. After the parameters we put the return
type. Collectively the parameters and the return type
are known as the function's signature.

Finally we have the function body which is a series of
statements between curly braces. In this body we invoke a built-in function called `panic` which causes a
run time error. (We'll see more about panic later in
this chapter) Writing functions can be difficult so it's a
good idea to break the process into manageable
chunks, rather than trying to implement the entire
thing in one large step.

Now lets take the code from our main function and
move it into our average function:

```
func average(xs []float64) float64 {
    total := 0.0
    for _, v := range xs {
        total += v
    }
    return total / float64(len(xs))
}
```

Notice that we changed the `fmt.Println` to be a `return`
instead. The return statement causes the function to
immediately stop and return the value after it to the

function that called this one. Modify `main` to look like this:

```
func main() {
    xs := []float64{98,93,77,82,83}
    fmt.Println(average(xs))
}
```

Running this program should give you exactly the same result as the original. A few things to keep in mind:

- The names of the parameters don't have to match in the calling function. For example we could have done this:

```
func main() {
    someOtherName := []float64{98,93,77,82,83}
    fmt.Println(average(someOtherName))
}
```

And our program would still work.

- Functions don't have access to anything in the calling function. This won't work:

```
func f() {
    fmt.Println(x)
}
func main() {
    x := 5
    f()
}
```

We need to either do this:

```
func f(x int) {
    fmt.Println(x)
}
func main() {
    x := 5
    f(x)
}
```

Or this:

```
var x int = 5
func f() {
    fmt.Println(x)
}
func main() {
    f()
}
```

- Functions are built up in a "stack". Suppose we had this program:

```go
func main() {
    fmt.Println(f1())
}
func f1() int {
    return f2()
}
func f2() int {
    return 1
}
```

We could visualize it like this:

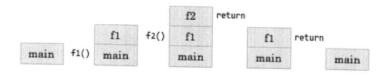

Each time we call a function we push it onto the call stack and each time we return from a function we pop the last function off of the stack.

- We can also name the return type:

```go
func f2() (r int) {
    r = 1
    return
}
```

7.2   Returning Multiple Values

Go is also capable of returning multiple values from a function:

```
func f() (int, int) {
    return 5, 6
}

func main() {
    x, y := f()
}
```

Three changes are necessary: change the return type to contain multiple types separated by `,`, change the expression after the return so that it contains multiple expressions separated by `,` and finally change the assignment statement so that multiple values are on the left side of the `:=` or `=`.

Multiple values are often used to return an error value along with the result (`x, err := f()`), or a boolean to indicate success (`x, ok := f()`).

7.3   Variadic Functions

There is a special form available for the last parameter in a Go function:

```
func add(args ...int) int {
    total := 0
    for _, v := range args {
        total += v
    }
    return total
}
func main() {
    fmt.Println(add(1,2,3))
}
```

By using ... before the type name of the last parameter you can indicate that it takes zero or more of those
parameters. In this case we take zero or more `int`s. We
invoke the function like any other function except we
can pass as many `int`s as we want.

This is precisely how the `fmt.Println` function is implemented:

```
func Println(a ...interface{}) (n int, err
error)
```

The `Println` function takes any number of values of
any type. (The special `interface{}` type will be discussed in more detail in chapter 9)

We can also pass a slice of `int`s by following the slice
with ...:

```
func main() {
    xs := []int{1,2,3}
    fmt.Println(add(xs...))
}
```

7.4   Closure

It is possible to create functions inside of functions:

```
func main() {
    add := func(x, y int) int {
        return x + y
    }
    fmt.Println(add(1,1))
}
```

`add` is a local variable that has the type `func(int, int)`
`int` (a function that takes two `int`s and returns an
`int`). When you create a local function like this it also
has access to other local variables (remember scope
from chapter 4):

```
func main() {
    x := 0
    increment := func() int {
        x++
        return x
    }
    fmt.Println(increment())
    fmt.Println(increment())
}
```

`increment` adds 1 to the variable `x` which is defined in the `main` function's scope. This `x` variable can be accessed and modified by the `increment` function. This is why the first time we call `increment` we see 1 displayed, but the second time we call it we see 2 displayed.

A function like this together with the non-local variables it references is known as a closure. In this case `increment` and the variable `x` form the closure.

One way to use closure is by writing a function which returns another function which − when called − can generate a sequence of numbers. For example here's how we might generate all the even numbers:

```
func makeEvenGenerator() func() uint {
    i := uint(0)
    return func() (ret uint) {
        ret = i
        i += 2
        return
    }
}
func main() {
    nextEven := makeEvenGenerator()
    fmt.Println(nextEven()) // 0
    fmt.Println(nextEven()) // 2
    fmt.Println(nextEven()) // 4
}
```

makeEvenGenerator returns a function which generates even numbers. Each time it's called it adds 2 to the local i variable which – unlike normal local variables – persists between calls.

7.5 Recursion

Finally a function is able to call itself. Here is one way to compute the factorial of a number:

```
func factorial(x uint) uint {
    if x == 0 {
        return 1
    }

    return x * factorial(x-1)
}
```

`factorial` calls itself, which is what makes this function recursive. In order to better understand how this function works, lets walk through `factorial(2)`:

- Is `x == 0`? No. (`x` is 2)
- Find the factorial of `x - 1`
  - Is `x == 0`? No. (`x` is 1)
  - Find the `factorial` of `x - 1`
    - Is `x == 0`? Yes, return 1.
  - return `1 * 1`
- return `2 * 1`

Closure and recursion are powerful programming techniques which form the basis of a paradigm known as functional programming. Most people will find functional programming more difficult to understand than an approach based on for loops, if statements, variables and simple functions.

7.6 Defer, Panic & Recover

Go has a special statement called `defer` which sched-
ules a function call to be run after the function completes. Consider the following example:

```
package main

import "fmt"

func first() {
    fmt.Println("1st")
}
func second() {
    fmt.Println("2nd")
}
func main() {
    defer second()
    first()
}
```

This program prints `1st` followed by `2nd`. Basically defer moves the call to `second` to the end of the function:

```
func main() {
    first()
    second()
}
```

`defer` is often used when resources need to be freed in
some way. For example when we open a file we need to

make sure to close it later. With `defer`:

```
f, _ := os.Open(filename)
defer f.Close()
```

This has 3 advantages: (1) it keeps our `Close` call near our `Open` call so its easier to understand, (2) if our function had multiple return statements (perhaps one in an `if` and one in an `else`) `Close` will happen before both of them and (3) deferred functions are run even if a run-time panic occurs.

Panic & Recover

Earlier we created a function that called the `panic` function to cause a run time error. We can handle a run-time panic with the built-in `recover` function. `recover` stops the panic and returns the value that was passed to the call to `panic`. We might be tempted to use it like this:

```
package main

import "fmt"

func main() {
    panic("PANIC")
    str := recover()
    fmt.Println(str)
}
```

But the call to recover will never happen in this case because the call to panic immediately stops execution of the function. Instead we have to pair it with defer:

```
package main

import "fmt"

func main() {
    defer func() {
        str := recover()
        fmt.Println(str)
    }()
    panic("PANIC")
}
```

A panic generally indicates a programmer error (for example attempting to access an index of an array that's out of bounds, forgetting to initialize a map, etc.) or an exceptional condition that there's no easy way to recover from. (Hence the name "panic")

Problems

1. `sum` is a function which takes a slice of numbers and adds them together. What would its function signature look like in Go?

2. Write a function which takes an integer and halves it and returns true if it was even or false if it was odd. For example `half(1)` should return `(0, false)` and `half(2)` should return `(1, true)`.

3. Write a function with one variadic parameter that finds the greatest number in a list of numbers.

4. Using `makeEvenGenerator` as an example, write a `makeOddGenerator` function that generates odd numbers.

5. The Fibonacci sequence is defined as: `fib(0) = 0`, `fib(1) = 1`, `fib(n) = fib(n-1) + fib(n-2)`. Write a recursive function which can find `fib(n)`.

6. What are defer, panic and recover? How do you recover from a run-time panic?

8   Pointers

When we call a function that takes an argument, that
argument is copied to the function:

```
func zero(x int) {
    x = 0
}
func main() {
    x := 5
    zero(x)
    fmt.Println(x) // x is still 5
}
```

In this program the zero function will not modify the
original x variable in the main function. But what if we
wanted to? One way to do this is to use a special data
type known as a pointer:

```
func zero(xPtr *int) {
    *xPtr = 0
}
func main() {
    x := 5
    zero(&x)
    fmt.Println(x) // x is 0
}
```

Pointers reference a location in memory where a value is stored rather than the value itself. (They point to something else) By using a pointer (`*int`) the `zero` function is able to modify the original variable.

8.1   The * and & operators

In Go a pointer is represented using the `*` (asterisk) character followed by the type of the stored value. In the `zero` function `xPtr` is a pointer to an `int`.

`*` is also used to "dereference" pointer variables. Dereferencing a pointer gives us access to the value the pointer points to. When we write `*xPtr = 0` we are saying "store the `int` 0 in the memory location `xPtr` refers to". If we try `xPtr = 0` instead we will get a compiler error because `xPtr` is not an `int` it's a `*int`, which can only be given another `*int`.

Finally we use the `&` operator to find the address of a

variable. &x returns a `*int` (pointer to an int) because x
is an `int`. This is what allows us to modify the original
variable. &x in `main` and `xPtr` in `zero` refer to the same
memory location.

8.2   new

Another way to get a pointer is to use the built-in `new`
function:

```go
func one(xPtr *int) {
    *xPtr = 1
}
func main() {
    xPtr := new(int)
    one(xPtr)
    fmt.Println(*xPtr) // x is 1
}
```

`new` takes a type as an argument, allocates enough
memory to fit a value of that type and returns a
pointer to it.

In some programming languages there is a significant
difference between using `new` and `&`, with great care being needed to eventually delete anything created with
`new`. Go is not like this, it's a garbage collected programming language which means memory is cleaned
up automatically when nothing refers to it anymore.

Pointers are rarely used with Go's built-in types, but as we will see in the next chapter, they are extremely useful when paired with structs.

Problems

1. How do you get the memory address of a variable?

2. How do you assign a value to a pointer?

3. How do you create a new pointer?

4. What is the value of x after running this program:

```
func square(x *float64) {
    *x = *x * *x
}
func main() {
    x := 1.5
    square(&x)
}
```

5. Write a program that can swap two integers (x := 1; y := 2; swap(&x, &y) should give you x=2 and y=1).

9 Structs and Interfaces

Although it would be possible for us to write programs only using Go's built-in data types, at some point it would become quite tedious. Consider a program that interacts with shapes:

```
package main

import ("fmt"; "math")

func distance(x1, y1, x2, y2 float64) float64 {
    a := x2 - x1
    b := y2 - y1
    return math.Sqrt(a*a + b*b)
}

func rectangleArea(x1, y1, x2, y2 float64)
float64 {
    l := distance(x1, y1, x1, y2)
    w := distance(x1, y1, x2, y1)
    return l * w
}

func circleArea(x, y, r float64) float64 {
    return math.Pi * r*r
}
```

```
func main() {
    var rx1, ry1 float64 = 0, 0
    var rx2, ry2 float64 = 10, 10
    var cx, cy, cr float64 = 0, 0, 5

    fmt.Println(rectangleArea(rx1, ry1, rx2,
ry2))
    fmt.Println(circleArea(cx, cy, cr))
}
```

Keeping track of all the coordinates makes it difficult to see what the program is doing and will likely lead to mistakes.

9.1 Structs

An easy way to make this program better is to use a struct. A struct is a type which contains named fields. For example we could represent a Circle like this:

```
type Circle struct {
    x float64
    y float64
    r float64
}
```

The `type` keyword introduces a new type. It's followed by the name of the type (`Circle`), the keyword `struct` to indicate that we are defining a `struct` type and a list of fields inside of curly braces. Each field has a

name and a type. Like with functions we can collapse
fields that have the same type:

```
type Circle struct {
    x, y, r float64
}
```

Initialization

We can create an instance of our new Circle type in a
variety of ways:

```
var c Circle
```

Like with other data types, this will create a local Circle variable that is by default set to zero. For a `struct`
zero means each of the fields is set to their correspond-
ing zero value (`0` for `int`s, `0.0` for `float`s, `""` for `string`s,
`nil` for pointers, ...) We can also use the new function:

```
c := new(Circle)
```

This allocates memory for all the fields, sets each of
them to their zero value and returns a pointer.
(`*Circle`) More often we want to give each of the fields
a value. We can do this in two ways. Like this:

```
c := Circle{x: 0, y: 0, r: 5}
```

Or we can leave off the field names if we know the order they were defined:

```
c := Circle{0, 0, 5}
```

Fields

We can access fields using the . operator:

```
fmt.Println(c.x, c.y, c.r)
c.x = 10
c.y = 5
```

Let's modify the `circleArea` function so that it uses a `Circle`:

```
func circleArea(c Circle) float64 {
    return math.Pi * c.r*c.r
}
```

In main we have:

```
c := Circle{0, 0, 5}
fmt.Println(circleArea(c))
```

One thing to remember is that arguments are always copied in Go. If we attempted to modify one of the fields inside of the `circleArea` function, it would not modify the original variable. Because of this we would typically write the function like this:

```
func circleArea(c *Circle) float64 {
    return math.Pi * c.r*c.r
}
```

And change main:

```
c := Circle{0, 0, 5}
fmt.Println(circleArea(&c))
```

9.2 Methods

Although this is better than the first version of this code, we can improve it significantly by using a special type of function known as a method:

```
func (c *Circle) area() float64 {
    return math.Pi * c.r*c.r
}
```

In between the keyword `func` and the name of the function we've added a "receiver". The receiver is like a parameter – it has a name and a type – but by creating the function in this way it allows us to call the function using the . operator:

```
fmt.Println(c.area())
```

This is much easier to read, we no longer need the & operator (Go automatically knows to pass a pointer to the circle for this method) and because this function can only be used with Circles we can rename the function to just area.

Let's do the same thing for the rectangle:

```
type Rectangle struct {
    x1, y1, x2, y2 float64
}

func (r *Rectangle) area() float64 {
    l := distance(r.x1, r.y1, r.x1, r.y2)
    w := distance(r.x1, r.y1, r.x2, r.y1)
    return l * w
}
```

main has:

```
r := Rectangle{0, 0, 10, 10}
fmt.Println(r.area())
```

Embedded Types

A struct's fields usually represent the has-a relationship. For example a `Circle` has a `radius`. Suppose we had a person struct:

```
type Person struct {
    Name string
}
func (p *Person) Talk() {
    fmt.Println("Hi, my name is", p.Name)
}
```

And we wanted to create a new `Android` struct. We could do this:

```
type Android struct {
    Person Person
    Model string
}
```

This would work, but we would rather say an Android *is a* Person, rather than an Android *has a* Person. Go supports relationships like this by using an embedded type. Also known as anonymous fields, embedded types look like this:

```
type Android struct {
    Person
    Model string
}
```

We use the type (`Person`) and don't give it a name.
When defined this way the `Person` struct can be accessed using the type name:

```
a := new(Android)
a.Person.Talk()
```

But we can also call any `Person` methods directly on
the `Android`:

```
a := new(Android)
a.Talk()
```

The is-a relationship works this way intuitively: People can talk, an android is a person, therefore an android can talk.

9.3   Interfaces

You may have noticed that we were able to name the
`Rectangle`'s `area` method the same thing as the `Circle`'s
`area` method. This was no accident. In both real life

and in programming, relationships like these are com-
monplace. Go has a way of making these accidental
similarities explicit through a type known as an Interface. Here is an example of a `Shape` interface:

```
type Shape interface {
    area() float64
}
```

Like a struct an interface is created using the `type`
keyword, followed by a name and the keyword
`interface`. But instead of defining fields, we define a
"method set". A method set is a list of methods that a
type must have in order to "implement" the interface.

In our case both `Rectangle` and `Circle` have area methods which return `float64`s so both types implement the
`Shape` interface. By itself this wouldn't be particularly
useful, but we can use interface types as arguments to
functions:

```
func totalArea(shapes ...Shape) float64 {
    var area float64
    for _, s := range shapes {
        area += s.area()
    }
    return area
}
```

We would call this function like this:

```
fmt.Println(totalArea(&c, &r))
```

Interfaces can also be used as fields:

```
type MultiShape struct {
    shapes []Shape
}
```

We can even turn `MultiShape` itself into a `Shape` by giving it an area method:

```
func (m *MultiShape) area() float64 {
    var area float64
    for _, s := range m.shapes {
        area += s.area()
    }
    return area
}
```

Now a `MultiShape` can contain `Circles`, `Rectangles` or even other `MultiShapes`.

Problems

1. What's the difference between a method and a function?

2. Why would you use an embedded anonymous field instead of a normal named field?

3. Add a new method to the `Shape` interface called `perimeter` which calculates the perimeter of a shape. Implement the method for `Circle` and `Rectangle`.

10 Concurrency

Large programs are often made up of many smaller sub-programs. For example a web server handles requests made from web browsers and serves up HTML web pages in response. Each request is handled like a small program.

It would be ideal for programs like these to be able to run their smaller components at the same time (in the case of the web server to handle multiple requests). Making progress on more than one task simultaneously is known as concurrency. Go has rich support for concurrency using goroutines and channels.

10.1 Goroutines

A goroutine is a function that is capable of running concurrently with other functions. To create a goroutine we use the keyword go followed by a function invocation:

```
package main

import "fmt"

func f(n int) {
    for i := 0; i < 10; i++ {
        fmt.Println(n, ":", i)
    }
}

func main() {
    go f(0)
    var input string
    fmt.Scanln(&input)
}
```

This program consists of two goroutines. The first goroutine is implicit and is the main function itself. The
second goroutine is created when we call `go f(0)`. Normally when we invoke a function our program will execute all the statements in a function and then return
to the next line following the invocation. With a goroutine we return immediately to the next line and don't
wait for the function to complete. This is why the call
to the `Scanln` function has been included; without it
the program would exit before being given the opportu-
nity to print all the numbers.

Goroutines are lightweight and we can easily create
thousands of them. We can modify our program to run
10 goroutines by doing this:

```
func main() {
    for i := 0; i < 10; i++ {
        go f(i)
    }
    var input string
    fmt.Scanln(&input)
}
```

You may have noticed that when you run this program
it seems to run the goroutines in order rather than simultaneously. Let's add some delay to the function using `time.Sleep` and `rand.Intn`:

```
package main

import (
    "fmt"
    "time"
    "math/rand"
)

func f(n int) {
    for i := 0; i < 10; i++ {
        fmt.Println(n, ":", i)
        amt := time.Duration(rand.Intn(250))
        time.Sleep(time.Millisecond * amt)
    }
}
```

```
func main() {
    for i := 0; i < 10; i++ {
        go f(i)
    }
    var input string
    fmt.Scanln(&input)
}
```

f prints out the numbers from 0 to 10, waiting between 0 and 250 ms after each one. The goroutines should now run simultaneously.

10.2 Channels

Channels provide a way for two goroutines to communicate with one another and synchronize their execution. Here is an example program using channels:

```
package main

import (
    "fmt"
    "time"
)

func pinger(c chan string) {
    for i := 0; ; i++ {
        c <- "ping"
    }
}
func printer(c chan string) {
    for {
        msg := <- c
        fmt.Println(msg)
        time.Sleep(time.Second * 1)
    }
}
func main() {
    var c chan string = make(chan string)

    go pinger(c)
    go printer(c)

    var input string
    fmt.Scanln(&input)
}
```

This program will print "ping" forever (hit enter to stop it). A channel type is represented with the keyword `chan` followed by the type of the things that are passed on the channel (in this case we are passing strings). The `<-` (left arrow) operator is used to send

and receive messages on the channel. `c <- "ping"`
means send `"ping"`. `msg := <- c` means receive a message and store it in `msg`. The `fmt` line could also have
been written like this: `fmt.Println(<-c)` in which case
we could remove the previous line.

Using a channel like this synchronizes the two goroutines. When `pinger` attempts to send a message on the
channel it will wait until `printer` is ready to receive
the message. (this is known as blocking) Let's add another sender to the program and see what happens.
Add this function:

```
func ponger(c chan string) {
    for i := 0; ; i++ {
        c <- "pong"
    }
}
```

And modify `main`:

```
func main() {
    var c chan string = make(chan string)

    go pinger(c)
    go ponger(c)
    go printer(c)

    var input string
    fmt.Scanln(&input)
}
```

The program will now take turns printing "ping" and "pong".

Channel Direction

We can specify a direction on a channel type thus restricting it to either sending or receiving. For example pinger's function signature can be changed to this:

```
func pinger(c chan<- string)
```

Now c can only be sent to. Attempting to receive from c will result in a compiler error. Similarly we can change printer to this:

```
func printer(c <-chan string)
```

A channel that doesn't have these restrictions is known as bi-directional. A bi-directional channel can be passed to a function that takes send-only or receive-only channels, but the reverse is not true.

Select

Go has a special statement called `select` which works like a `switch` but for channels:

```go
func main() {
    c1 := make(chan string)
    c2 := make(chan string)

    go func() {
        for {
            c1 <- "from 1"
            time.Sleep(time.Second * 2)
        }
    }()
    go func() {
        for {
            c2 <- "from 2"
            time.Sleep(time.Second * 3)
        }
    }()
    go func() {
        for {
            select {
            case msg1 := <- c1:
                fmt.Println(msg1)
            case msg2 := <- c2:
                fmt.Println(msg2)
            }
        }
    }()

    var input string
    fmt.Scanln(&input)
}
```

This program prints "from 1" every 2 seconds and
"from 2" every 3 seconds. `select` picks the first channel
that is ready and receives from it (or sends to it). If

more than one of the channels are ready then it randomly picks which one to receive from. If none of the channels are ready, the statement blocks until one becomes available.

The `select` statement is often used to implement a timeout:

```
select {
case msg1 := <- c1:
    fmt.Println("Message 1", msg1)
case msg2 := <- c2:
    fmt.Println("Message 2", msg2)
case <- time.After(time.Second):
    fmt.Println("timeout")
}
```

`time.After` creates a channel and after the given duration will send the current time on it. (we weren't interested in the time so we didn't store it in a variable) We can also specify a `default` case:

```
select {
case msg1 := <- c1:
    fmt.Println("Message 1", msg1)
case msg2 := <- c2:
    fmt.Println("Message 2", msg2)
case <- time.After(time.Second):
    fmt.Println("timeout")
default:
    fmt.Println("nothing ready")
}
```

The default case happens immediately if none of the channels are ready.

Buffered Channels

It's also possible to pass a second parameter to the make function when creating a channel:

```
c := make(chan int, 1)
```

This creates a buffered channel with a capacity of 1. Normally channels are synchronous; both sides of the channel will wait until the other side is ready. A buffered channel is asynchronous; sending or receiving a message will not wait unless the channel is already full.

Problems

1. How do you specify the direction of a channel type?

2. Write your own `Sleep` function using `time.After`.

3. What is a buffered channel? How would you create one with a capacity of 20?

11 Packages

Go was designed to be a language that encourages good software engineering practices. An important part of high quality software is code reuse – embodied in the principle "Don't Repeat Yourself."

As we saw in chapter 7 functions are the first layer we turn to allow code reuse. Go also provides another mechanism for code reuse: packages. Nearly every program we've seen so far included this line:

```
import "fmt"
```

fmt is the name of a package that includes a variety of functions related to formatting and output to the screen. Bundling code in this way serves 3 purposes:

1. It reduces the chance of having overlapping names. This keeps our function names short and succinct

2. It organizes code so that its easier to find code

you want to reuse.

3. It speeds up the compiler by only requiring re-
   compilation of smaller chunks of a program. Although we use the package `fmt`, we don't have to
   recompile it every time we change our program.

11.1 Creating Packages

Packages only really make sense in the context of a
separate program which uses them. Without this separate program we have no way of using the package we
create. Let's create an application that will use a package we will write. Create a folder in `~/Go/src/golang-`
`book` called `chapter11`. Inside that folder create a file
called `main.go` which contains this:

```
package main

import "fmt"
import "golang-book/chapter11/math"

func main() {
    xs := []float64{1,2,3,4}
    avg := math.Average(xs)
    fmt.Println(avg)
}
```

Now create another folder inside of the `chapter11`

folder called math. Inside of this folder create a file called math.go that contains this:

```
package math

func Average(xs []float64) float64 {
    total := float64(0)
    for _, x := range xs {
        total += x
    }
    return total / float64(len(xs))
}
```

Using a terminal in the math folder you just created run go install. This will compile the math.go program and create a linkable object file: ~/Go/pkg/os_arch/golang-book/chapter11/math.a. (where os is something like windows and arch is something like amd64)

Now go back to the chapter11 folder and run go run main.go. You should see 2.5. Some things to note:

1. math is the name of a package that is part of Go's standard distribution, but since Go packages can be hierarchical we are safe to use the same name for our package. (The real math package is just math, ours is golang-book/chapter11/math)

2. When we import our math library we use its full name (`import` `"golang-book/chapter11/math"`), but inside of the `math.go` file we only use the last part of the name (`package math`).

3. We also only use the short name `math` when we reference functions from our library. If we wanted to use both libraries in the same program Go allows us to use an alias:

```
import m "golang-book/chapter11/math"

func main() {
    xs := []float64{1,2,3,4}
    avg := m.Average(xs)
    fmt.Println(avg)
}
```

`m` is the alias.

4. You may have noticed that every function in the packages we've seen start with a capital letter. In Go if something starts with a capital letter that means other packages (and programs) are able to see it. If we had named the function `average` instead of `Average` our `main` program would not have been able to see it.

It's a good practice to only expose the parts of

our package that we want other packages using and hide everything else. This allows us to freely change those parts later without having to worry about breaking other programs, and it makes our package easier to use.

5. Package names match the folders they fall in. There are ways around this, but it's a lot easier if you stay within this pattern.

11.2 Documentation

Go has the ability to automatically generate documentation for packages we write in a similar way to the standard package documentation. In a terminal run this command:

```
godoc golang-book/chapter11/math Average
```

You should see information displayed for the function we just wrote. We can improve this documentation by adding a comment before the function:

```
// Finds the average of a series of numbers
func Average(xs []float64) float64 {
```

If you run go install in the math folder, then re-run

the godoc command you should see our comment below the function definition. This documentation is also available in web form by running this command:

```
godoc -http=":6060"
```

and entering this URL into your browser:

```
http://localhost:6060/pkg/
```

You should be able to browse through all of the packages installed on your system.

Problems

1. Why do we use packages?

2. What is the difference between an identifier that starts with a capital letter and one which doesn't? (`Average` vs `average`)

3. What is a package alias? How do you make one?

4. We copied the average function from chapter 7 to our new package. Create `Min` and `Max` functions which find the minimum and maximum values in a slice of `float64`s.

5. How would you document the functions you created in #3?

12 Testing

Programming is not easy; even the best programmers are incapable of writing programs that work exactly as intended every time. Therefore an important part of the software development process is testing. Writing tests for our code is a good way to ensure quality and improve reliability.

Go includes a special program that makes writing tests easier, so let's create some tests for the package we made in the last chapter. In the `math` folder from `chapter11` create a new file called `math_test.go` that contains this:

```
package math

import "testing"

func TestAverage(t *testing.T) {
    var v float64
    v = Average([]float64{1,2})
    if v != 1.5 {
        t.Error("Expected 1.5, got ", v)
    }
}
```

Now run this command:

```
go test
```

You should see this:

```
$ go test
PASS
ok      golang-book/chapter11/math      0.032s
```

The `go test` command will look for any tests in any of
the files in the current folder and run them. Tests are
identified by starting a function with the word `Test`
and taking one argument of type `*testing.T`. In our
case since we're testing the `Average` function we name
the test function `TestAverage`.

Once we have the testing function setup we write tests
that use the code we're testing. In this case we know
the average of [1,2] should be 1.5 so that's what we
check. It's probably a good idea to test many different
combinations of numbers so let's change our test program a little:

```
package math

import "testing"

type testpair struct {
    values []float64
    average float64
}

var tests = []testpair{
    { []float64{1,2}, 1.5 },
    { []float64{1,1,1,1,1,1}, 1 },
    { []float64{-1,1}, 0 },
}

func TestAverage(t *testing.T) {
    for _, pair := range tests {
        v := Average(pair.values)
        if v != pair.average {
            t.Error(
                "For", pair.values,
                "expected", pair.average,
                "got", v,
            )
        }
    }
}
```

This is a very common way to setup tests (abundant examples can be found in the source code for the packages included with Go). We create a `struct` to represent the inputs and outputs for the function. Then we create a list of these `struct`s (pairs). Then we loop through each one and run the function.

Problems

1. Writing a good suite of tests is not always easy,
   but the process of writings tests often reveals
   more about a problem then you may at first re-
   alize. For example, with our `Average` function
   what happens if you pass in an empty list
   (`[]float64{}`)? How could we modify the function to return `0` in this case?

2. Write a series of tests for the `Min` and `Max` functions you wrote in the previous chapter.

13 The Core Packages

Instead of writing everything from scratch, most real world programming depends on our ability to interface with existing libraries. This chapter will take a look at some of the most commonly used packages included with Go.

First a word of warning: although some of these libraries are fairly obvious (or have been explained in previous chapters), many of the libraries included with Go require specialized domain specific knowledge (for example: cryptography). It is beyond the scope of this book to explain these underlying technologies.

13.1 Strings

Go includes a large number of functions to work with strings in the `strings` package:

```
package main

import (
    "fmt"
    "strings"
)

func main() {
    fmt.Println(
        // true
        strings.Contains("test", "es"),

        // 2
        strings.Count("test", "t"),

        // true
        strings.HasPrefix("test", "te"),

        // true
        strings.HasSuffix("test", "st"),

        // 1
        strings.Index("test", "e"),

        // "a-b"
        strings.Join([]string{"a","b"}, "-"),

        // == "aaaaa"
        strings.Repeat("a", 5),

        // "bbaa"
        strings.Replace("aaaa", "a", "b", 2),

        // []string{"a","b","c","d","e"}
        strings.Split("a-b-c-d-e", "-"),
```

```
        // "test"
        strings.ToLower("TEST"),

        // "TEST"
        strings.ToUpper("test"),

    )
}
```

Sometimes we need to work with strings as binary data. To convert a string to a slice of bytes (and vice-versa) do this:

```
arr := []byte("test")
str := string([]byte{'t','e','s','t'})
```

13.2 Input / Output

Before we look at files we need to understand Go's io package. The io package consists of a few functions, but mostly interfaces used in other packages. The two main interfaces are Reader and Writer. Readers support reading via the Read method. Writers support writing via the Write method. Many functions in Go take Readers or Writers as arguments. For example the io package has a Copy function which copies data from a Reader to a Writer:

```
func Copy(dst Writer, src Reader) (written
int64, err error)
```

To read or write to a `[]byte` or a `string` you can use the `Buffer` struct found in the `bytes` package:

```
var buf bytes.Buffer
buf.Write([]byte("test"))
```

A `Buffer` doesn't have to be initialized and supports both the `Reader` and `Writer` interfaces. You can convert it into a `[]byte` by calling `buf.Bytes()`. If you only need to read from a string you can also use the `strings.NewReader` function which is more efficient than using a buffer.

13.3 Files & Folders

To open a file in Go use the `Open` function from the `os` package. Here is an example of how to read the contents of a file and display them on the terminal:

```go
package main

import (
    "fmt"
    "os"
)

func main() {
    file, err := os.Open("test.txt")
    if err != nil {
        // handle the error here
        return
    }
    defer file.Close()

    // get the file size
    stat, err := file.Stat()
    if err != nil {
        return
    }

    // read the file
    bs := make([]byte, stat.Size())
    _, err = file.Read(bs)
    if err != nil {
        return
    }

    str := string(bs)
    fmt.Println(str)
}
```

We use `defer file.Close()` right after opening the file to make sure the file is closed as soon as the function completes. Reading files is very common, so there's a shorter way to do this:

```go
package main

import (
    "fmt"
    "io/ioutil"
)

func main() {
    bs, err := ioutil.ReadFile("test.txt")
    if err != nil {
        return
    }
    str := string(bs)
    fmt.Println(str)
}
```

Here is how we can create a file:

```
package main

import (
    "os"
)

func main() {
    file, err := os.Create("test.txt")
    if err != nil {
        // handle the error here
        return
    }
    defer file.Close()

    file.WriteString("test")
}
```

To get the contents of a directory we use the same `os.Open` function but give it a directory path instead of a file name. Then we call the `Readdir` method:

```
package main

import (
    "fmt"
    "os"
)

func main() {
    dir, err := os.Open(".")
    if err != nil {
        return
    }
    defer dir.Close()

    fileInfos, err := dir.Readdir(-1)
    if err != nil {
        return
    }
    for _, fi := range fileInfos {
        fmt.Println(fi.Name())
    }
}
```

Often we want to recursively walk a folder (read the folder's contents, all the sub-folders, all the sub-sub-folders, ...). To make this easier there's a `Walk` function provided in the `path/filepath` package:

```
package main

import (
    "fmt"
    "os"
    "path/filepath"
)

func main() {
    filepath.Walk(".", func(path string, info
os.FileInfo, err error) error {
        fmt.Println(path)
        return nil
    })
}
```

The function you pass to Walk is called for every file
and folder in the root folder. (in this case .)

13.4 Errors

Go has a built-in type for errors that we have already
seen (the error type). We can create our own errors by
using the New function in the errors package:

```
package main

import "errors"

func main() {
    err := errors.New("error message")
}
```

13.5 Containers & Sort

In addition to lists and maps Go has several more collections available underneath the container package. We'll take a look at the `container/list` package as an example.

List

The `container/list` package implements a doubly-linked list. A linked list is a type of data structure that looks like this:

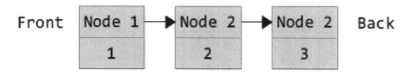

Each node of the list contains a value (1, 2, or 3 in this case) and a pointer to the next node. Since this is a doubly-linked list each node will also have pointers to the previous node. This list could be created by this program:

```
package main

import ("fmt" ; "container/list")

func main() {
    var x list.List
    x.PushBack(1)
    x.PushBack(2)
    x.PushBack(3)

    for e := x.Front(); e != nil; e=e.Next() {
        fmt.Println(e.Value.(int))
    }
}
```

The zero value for a `List` is an empty list (a `*List` can also be created using `list.New`). Values are appended to the list using `PushBack`. We loop over each item in the list by getting the first element, and following all the links until we reach nil.

Sort

The sort package contains functions for sorting arbitrary data. There are several predefined sorting functions (for slices of ints and floats) Here's an example for how to sort your own data:

```
package main

import ("fmt" ; "sort")

type Person struct {
    Name string
    Age int
}

type ByName []Person

func (this ByName) Len() int {
    return len(this)
}
func (this ByName) Less(i, j int) bool {
    return this[i].Name < this[j].Name
}
func (this ByName) Swap(i, j int) {
    this[i], this[j] = this[j], this[i]
}

func main() {
    kids := []Person{
        {"Jill",9},
        {"Jack",10},
    }
    sort.Sort(ByName(kids))
    fmt.Println(kids)
}
```

The `Sort` function in `sort` takes a `sort.Interface` and sorts it. The `sort.Interface` requires 3 methods: `Len`, `Less` and `Swap`. To define our own sort we create a new type (`ByName`) and make it equivalent to a slice of what we want to sort. We then define the 3 methods.

Sorting our list of people is then as easy as casting the list into our new type. We could also sort by age by doing this:

```
type ByAge []Person
func (this ByAge) Len() int {
    return len(this)
}
func (this ByAge) Less(i, j int) bool {
    return this[i].Age < this[j].Age
}
func (this ByAge) Swap(i, j int) {
    this[i], this[j] = this[j], this[i]
}
```

13.6 Hashes & Cryptography

A hash function takes a set of data and reduces it to a smaller fixed size. Hashes are frequently used in programming for everything from looking up data to easily detecting changes. Hash functions in Go are broken into two categories: cryptographic and non-cryptographic.

The non-cryptographic hash functions can be found underneath the hash package and include adler32, crc32, crc64 and fnv. Here's an example using crc32:

```
package main

import (
    "fmt"
    "hash/crc32"
)

func main() {
    h := crc32.NewIEEE()
    h.Write([]byte("test"))
    v := h.Sum32()
    fmt.Println(v)
}
```

The `crc32` hash object implements the `Writer` inter-face, so we can write bytes to it like any other `Writer`. Once we've written everything we want we call `Sum32()` to return a `uint32`. A common use for `crc32` is to compare two files. If the `Sum32` value for both files is the same, it's highly likely (though not 100% certain) that the files are the same. If the values are different then the files are definitely not the same:

```
package main

import (
    "fmt"
    "hash/crc32"
    "io/ioutil"
)

func getHash(filename string) (uint32, error) {

    bs, err := ioutil.ReadFile("test1.txt")
    if err != nil {
        return 0, err
    }
    h := crc32.NewIEEE()
    h.Write(bs)
    return h.Sum32(), nil
}

func main() {
    h1, err := getHash("test1.txt")
    if err != nil {
        return
    }
    h2, err := getHash("test2.txt")
    if err != nil {
        return
    }
    fmt.Println(h1, h2, h1 == h2)
}
```

Cryptographic hash functions are similar to their non-cryptographic counterparts, but they have the added property of being hard to reverse. Given the cryptographic hash of a set of data, it's extremely difficult to

determine what made the hash. These hashes are often used in security applications.

One common cryptographic hash function is known as
SHA-1. Here's how it is used:

```
package main

import (
    "fmt"
    "crypto/sha1"
)

func main() {
    h := sha1.New()
    h.Write([]byte("test"))
    bs := h.Sum([]byte{})
    fmt.Println(bs)
}
```

This example is very similar to the `crc32` one, because
both `crc32` and `sha1` implement the `hash.Hash` interface. The main difference is that whereas `crc32` computes a 32 bit hash, `sha1` computes a 160 bit hash.
There is no native type to represent a 160 bit number,
so we use a slice of 20 bytes instead.

13.7 Servers

Writing network servers in Go is very easy. We will

first take a look at how to create a TCP server:

```go
package main

import (
    "encoding/gob"
    "fmt"
    "net"
)

func server() {
    // listen on a port
    ln, err := net.Listen("tcp", ":9999")
    if err != nil {
        fmt.Println(err)
        return
    }
    for {
        // accept a connection
        c, err := ln.Accept()
        if err != nil {
            fmt.Println(err)
            continue
        }
        // handle the connection
        go handleServerConnection(c)
    }
}
```

```go
func handleServerConnection(c net.Conn) {
    // receive the message
    var msg string
    err := gob.NewDecoder(c).Decode(&msg)
    if err != nil {
        fmt.Println(err)
    } else {
        fmt.Println("Received", msg)
    }

    c.Close()
}

func client() {
    // connect to the server
    c, err := net.Dial("tcp", "127.0.0.1:9999")
    if err != nil {
        fmt.Println(err)
        return
    }

    // send the message
    msg := "Hello World"
    fmt.Println("Sending", msg)
    err = gob.NewEncoder(c).Encode(msg)
    if err != nil {
        fmt.Println(err)
    }

    c.Close()
}
```

```
func main() {
    go server()
    go client()

    var input string
    fmt.Scanln(&input)
}
```

This example uses the `encoding/gob` package which makes it easy to encode Go values so that other Go programs (or the same Go program in this case) can read them. Additional encodings are available in packages underneath `encoding` (like `encoding/json`) as well as in 3rd party packages. (for example we could use `labix.org/v2/mgo/bson` for bson support)

HTTP

HTTP servers are even easier to setup and use:

```
package main

import ("net/http" ; "io")

func hello(res http.ResponseWriter, req
*http.Request) {
    res.Header().Set(
        "Content-Type",
        "text/html",
    )
    io.WriteString(
        res,
        `<doctype html>
<html>
    <head>
        <title>Hello World</title>
    </head>
    <body>
        Hello World!
    </body>
</html>`,
    )
}

func main() {
    http.HandleFunc("/hello", hello)
    http.ListenAndServe(":9000", nil)
}
```

HandleFunc handles a URL route (/hello) by calling the
given function. We can also handle static files by using
FileServer:

```
http.Handle(
    "/assets/",
    http.StripPrefix(
        "/assets/",
        http.FileServer(http.Dir("assets"))),
    ),
)
```

RPC

The `net/rpc` (remote procedure call) and
`net/rpc/jsonrpc` packages provide an easy way to expose methods so they can be invoked over a network.
(rather than just in the program running them)

```go
package main

import (
    "fmt"
    "net"
    "net/rpc"
)

type Server struct {}
func (this *Server) Negate(i int64, reply
*int64) error {
    *reply = -i
    return nil
}

func server() {
    rpc.Register(new(Server))
    ln, err := net.Listen("tcp", ":9999")
    if err != nil {
        fmt.Println(err)
        return
    }
    for {
        c, err := ln.Accept()
        if err != nil {
            continue
        }
        go rpc.ServeConn(c)
    }
}
```

```
func client() {
    c, err := rpc.Dial("tcp", "127.0.0.1:9999")
    if err != nil {
        fmt.Println(err)
        return
    }
    var result int64
    err = c.Call("Server.Negate", int64(999),
&result)
    if err != nil {
        fmt.Println(err)
    } else {
        fmt.Println("Server.Negate(999) =",
result)
    }
}

func main() {
    go server()
    go client()

    var input string
    fmt.Scanln(&input)
}
```

This program is similar to the TCP example, except now we created an object to hold all the methods we want to expose and we call the Negate method from the client. See the documentation in net/rpc for more details.

13.8 Parsing Command Line Arguments

When we invoke a command on the terminal it's possible to pass that command arguments. We've seen this
with the `go` command:

```
go run myfile.go
```

run and myfile.go are arguments. We can also pass
flags to a command:

```
go run -v myfile.go
```

The flag package allows us to parse arguments and
flags sent to our program. Here's an example program
that generates a number between 0 and 6. We can
change the max value by sending a flag (`-max=100`) to
the program:

```
package main

import ("fmt";"flag";"math/rand")

func main() {
    // Define flags
    maxp := flag.Int("max", 6, "the max value")
    // Parse
    flag.Parse()
    // Generate a number between 0 and max
    fmt.Println(rand.Intn(*maxp))
}
```

Any additional non-flag arguments can be retrieved with `flag.Args()` which returns a `[]string`.

13.9 Synchronization Primitives

The preferred way to handle concurrency and synchronization in Go is through goroutines and channels as discussed in chapter 10. However Go does provide more traditional multithreading routines in the `sync` and `sync/atomic` packages.

Mutexes

A mutex (mutal exclusive lock) locks a section of code to a single thread at a time and is used to protect shared resources from non-atomic operations. Here is an example of a mutex:

```go
package main

import (
    "fmt"
    "sync"
    "time"
)
func main() {
    m := new(sync.Mutex)

    for i := 0; i < 10; i++ {
        go func(i int) {
            m.Lock()
            fmt.Println(i, "start")
            time.Sleep(time.Second)
            fmt.Println(i, "end")
            m.Unlock()
        }(i)
    }

    var input string
    fmt.Scanln(&input)
}
```

When the mutex (m) is locked any other attempt to lock it will block until it is unlocked. Great care should be taken when using mutexes or the synchronization primitives provided in the `sync/atomic` package.

Traditional multithreaded programming is difficult; it's easy to make mistakes and those mistakes are hard to find, since they may depend on a very specific, relatively rare, and difficult to reproduce set of circumstances. One of Go's biggest strengths is that the concurrency features it provides are much easier to understand and use properly than threads and locks.

14 Next Steps

We now have all the information we need to write most Go programs. But it would be dangerous to conclude that therefore we are competent programmers. Programming is as much a craft as it is just having knowledge. This chapter will provide you with some suggestions about how best to master the craft of programming.

14.1 Study the Masters

Part of becoming a good artist or writer is studying the works of the masters. It's no different with programming. One of the best ways to become a skilled programmer is to study the source code produced by others. Go is well suited to this task since the source code for the entire project is freely available.

For example we might take a look at the source code to the `io/util` library available at:

http://golang.org/src/pkg/io/ioutil/ioutil.go

Read the code slowly and deliberately. Try to understand every line and read the supplied comments. For example in the `ReadFile` method there's a comment that says this:

```
// It's a good but not certain bet that FileInfo
// will tell us exactly how much to read, so
// let's try it but be prepared for the answer
// to be wrong.
```

This method probably started out simpler than what it became so this is a great example of how programs can evolve after testing and why it's important to supply comments with those changes. All of the source code for all of the packages is available at:

http://golang.org/src/pkg/

14.2 Make Something

One of the best ways to hone your skills is to practice coding. There are a lot of ways to do this: You could work on challenging programming problems from sites like Project Euler (http://projecteuler.net/) or try your hand at a larger project. Perhaps try to implement a web server or write a simple game.